A Nail the Evening Hangs On

Monica Sok

A Nail the Evening Hangs On

Copper Canyon Press

Port Townsend, Washington

Cover art: Bun Em's Silk. Photograph by Hieu Minh Nguyen.

Copper Canyon Press is in residence at Fort Worden State Park in Port Townsend, Washington, under the auspices of Centrum. Centrum is a gathering place for artists and creative thinkers from around the world, students of all ages and backgrounds, and audiences seeking extraordinary cultural enrichment.

LIBRARY OF CONGRESS CATALOGING-IN-PUBLICATION DATA

Names: Sok, Monica, 1990– author.

Title: A nail the evening hangs on / Monica Sok.

Description: Port Townsend, Washington : Copper Canyon Press, [2020]

Identifiers: LCCN 2019019607 | ISBN 9781556595608 (pbk. : alk. paper)

Classification: LCC PS3619.O39 A6 2020 | DDC 811/.6—dc23

LC record available at https://lccn.loc.gov/2019019607

9 8 7 6 5 4 3 2 FIRST PRINTING

COPPER CANYON PRESS

Post Office Box 271

Port Townsend, Washington 98368

www.coppercanyonpress.org

for Bun Em

Contents

A Nail the Evening Hangs On

I

Ask the Locals

Nobody knows: How those so-called revolutionaries
who wanted so-called Year Zero so bad,
turned into mosquitoes. I mean, mosquitoes, right?
Because not butterflies or moths rolling
in the mass graves—we all know the moths are children
who didn't make it past five. My theory is those creeps
suck the blood of their victims to forget
with their bare hands or with other kinds of hands,
the kinds with teeth. They forgot. Don't forget: If you
scratch your arms like that, a huge welt will appear—
a rash, and those mosquitoes will keep coming.
You heard it from me. Don't scratch their real names.
Toothpaste over that bump won't soothe you,
not this one. I'll tell you something personal: Every time
I hear their real names, I itch my skin. I itch my own name
too. *Mosquitoes.* Call them *mosquitoes.* This kind keeps going
like that mosquito's straw on your calf keeps sucking.
This is when I tell you: Don't bend.
Slap.

Americans Dancing in the Heart of Darkness

It's the Water Festival, the city is a crowd. My skin full of sun
like so many country people who have come to Phnom Penh.

The Americans hate me and I hate them,
but they're the only students with me and maybe I'm American too.

When I return to my windowless room at the Golden Gate Hotel,
I order fresh young coconut, a club sandwich, and French fries.

A woman with a bruised face and a silver tray walks up seven floors,
knocks on my door. The exchange students order room service too,

and the same woman walks the flights of stairs nine more times.
Fireworks crackle and I think, *I'll be back to this same festival with my family.*

In the morning, thirty missed calls. There has been a human stampede
on the bridge to Koh Pich—347 reported dead, 755 injured.

Shoes litter the river. The exchange program advises us to stay away
from Diamond Island. The prime minister's remarks: *This is the worst thing*

to happen since the Khmer Rouge. The Americans agree.
I grow quiet in my windowless room. I step outside for air.

The city, a crowd disappearing. The crowd, evacuated to the provinces.
Cambodia, a perpetual stampede.

School canceled at the university—a funerary ceremony instead.
Do the Americans understand the program director when she tells us

her neighbor's son has died? Most likely not. Later that evening
they still don't understand, but I go with them anyway

to the Heart of Darkness, the nightclub empty but open.
We dance with Khmer boys. Strobe lights pull us on the floor. This way.

That. Our feet grope the shiny, black tiles reflecting the bar
where old expats sit with Khmer women making money. *Yeah, yeah.*

It isn't expensive to get here or get back. We tuk-a-tuk-tuk and we dance. They laugh.
Meanwhile my mother calls me. My father calls me. My auntie calls me

from Prek Eng. My uncle down the street from the hotel.
My uncle in Kandal. My cousin's uncle in Siem Reap.

The Radio Host Goes into Hiding

Disguising myself as old people

      to survive in these fields of black-uniformed Khmer   red-white krama
        our outlined rib cages and tight skin
                    if I could air
          the voices of the people   to the Powers of the world
                what would they say
about the Khmer Rouge   would we throw our fists
       Angkar is everything we shout
              everything
   we the old people
        allowed   saucepans
new people only possess   spoons   to dig more than eat
                  what a society

*

I was warned by the French
                    before they left Kampuchea   in a hurry
        Come with us they said   but like my only friend Rithisal
                              I chose not to abandon
    in such cowardly fashion

                    Rithisal young historian says
    why the Powers do nothing to end this experiment
    first began with American president orders from menu
                campaign   breakfast   lunch   dinner
snack on Ho Chi Minh Trail   Kampuchea after independence
                not land
        for wars   Khmer Rouge in power   threatens
Phnom Penh evacuate now
                the city will be bombed   I say quiet Rithisal not so loud

                              *

in the fields

I rehearse alone

in my thoughts   in Phnom Penh my job was cyclo driver

cyclo driver cyclo driver

see my legs so strong   my skin dark from sun

born in Battambang

cyclo cyclo cyclo cyclo

almost humming Yol Aularong aloud

but Rithisal heard whispers the song is dead

*

much time passing no radio
to tell world news or hear news of world

hello welcome to Year Zero Public Radio we are on air
my confession
I among the new people
act as the old people
I among the old people once lived
as new people

I among enemy
am enemy

*

at night I stand close to Angkar leaders
who invite us to their meetings   in loudspeaker

                                the village chief speaks   in slogans
                but

like water to survive   I must hold on to   an individual idea
        to keep strong   because
to be reeducated is to be destroyed
                                        the sweet potato
                        a young girl plants in the ground
five miles from the village commune
she does not know I am watching
                                she hums an Angkar
                                        song walking home

*

Rithisal

                    his wife Rachana   a singer

     which camp is she   we don't know

                her voice like milk when she sang

      in secret Rithisal writes what leaders say or do

records the tortured   witnesses young man hands tied eyes plead

stare straight into gun barrel   floating in river

not so loud Rithisal not here

                         think of Rachana I say

        but leaders suspect

                      Rithisal and me   then send us to a place

called Tuol Sleng   he whispers his kids used to go to school here

            and where is Rachana   looks away

                     *

we enter I forget which day   but it is Year Zero   the place Tuol Sleng
         a prison   people locked in stalls   old people new people Khmer Rouge
maybe Pol Pot himself   instruments of torture in the schoolyard
                  Rithisal writes won't listen to me he writes
I ask him if he thinks his children are Angkar's children now
         he raises a fist says *Whoever opposes*
         Angkar is a corpse   Angkar never
              makes mistakes   Angkar
                      is everything   Angkar cares for

                                        us all

                             *

these fields   rice paddies land mines mass graves bodies bodies
no votes for ancient wonder of the world   Rithisal takes notes on
        medicinal experiments executions force-feed excrement forced confessions
                            babies thrown
                                    then in the air
        Rithisal tells me all the missing pictures
                            quiet not so loud here not here not so loud

not here not here not here not here

                                *

on air on air Year Zero Public Radio
what time is it what day is it

Year Zero   everyone gone

Rithisal gone   never see him again

world   can you hear me   can you hear me
find the sweet potato
in a hole dug up
look for the girl   who planted it there

Sestina

There's a sister who works so hard she never talks.
A sister who screams when she hears dogs bark.
A sister whose breasts have grown dry. A sister who always hides.
There's a time comrades come to the hut.
They can't tell who's who—How many are you?
Where's the other one hiding? That sister stays close,

somewhere in a hole, closed off with dirt.
Sometimes she sits with the sister whose baby lacked milk.
In her place of hiding, she cries, thinks of comforting words
but her mouth goes dry. In a far village,
where works the sister who never talks: the sunset.
Finally, it's her chance. Time to run back,

but this time an owl screeches. She closes her eyes.
She disappears, pretends she's the one who can fly.
That sister so quiet. How does that sister stay quiet?
Biting her lips she goes into hiding: between her teeth,
the skin of a snake, hiding like a chasm in a field, a hole
in the door to spy on the time, dark knot

high up in a greasy tree, little dry well in a forgotten yard
where sounds of smoke and fighting drive close.
One sister soils her sarong. To wash it, the sisters search for water
but find, full of air, a balloon which swollen in the river
makes the youngest scream and cry, she who holds hands
walking around the open eyes, her own face hiding.

Then the sister who never speaks begins to speak.
I want to go home, she says. But home is not close at all.
No salty plum juice, no rice, or fish dried.
That dream is dry. And tracing with a stick,
a sister who closes a circle around them in the dirt,
hiding them safely inside—This is a circle,

a time warp around us sisters, so we can go back
to when we girls were not hiding, when fear didn't dry us up,
and we could be whoever we were, dear sisters.

The Weaver

She threaded the loom
with one strand of her long silver hair,
which might have kept growing until she was done,
which might have fallen out
but I would come in and
sit beside her on the cushion, without her noticing,
and she would continue.
Every day I saw this old woman
weaving at her loom, rivers and lakes
underneath her hair.
The bottom full of silt.
I could see it if I reached with a comb
and that was when she'd look at me.
Under her hair
she kept her oldest son,
who was out for a morning swim
with swallows swooping down to touch
the water. It made her happy
as she worked on silk dresses
and her hair never ran out.
Sometimes, when she was tired,
she'd tie it up
and let all the tired animals around her house
drink from her head.

Recurring Dreams

0

It was a strange dinner. His empty chair.
My brother missing. Didn't ask my parents questions.

The old house. Didn't ask why.

The wooden table the kitchen cramped.
My back against the wall. I sucked in my belly.
My father rationed more food.

Ate as much as I could. My mother's soup.
Rice on my plate. She took me to the bus.
He went to work. I went to another country.

Off the last stop. In the fields. Workers gathering grain.
Black pajamas.

Someone I knew.

I ran home. In the kitchen. Found her.

What are you doing here?
Before she took me back. She said.
You must know. Your history.

I

It was a very strange dinner. I tried to ask
my parents questions. The wooden table,
the kitchen cramped. My father spooned more rice on my plate.

I went to another country, where workers
were gathering grain. *What are you doing here?*
You must know.

II

His empty chair in the old house. My back against the wall.
I ate as much as I could. She took me to the bus after dinner.
Off the last stop, they gave me black pajamas.

In the kitchen, before she took me back, she said—

III

My brother is missing. I don't need to ask why. I suck in my belly,
wanting my mother's soup. He went to work in the fields.
Someone found her, he said. *What are you doing here?*

Self-Portrait in Siem Reap

The French chef says, *Try the foie gras, it's very good.*
So I treat myself to the liver of a force-fed goose.

Give it to me on a crostini with black currant!
In America, I don't get to do this sort of rich-people thing.

The waiter tells me he was a translator for Angelina Jolie,
saw her roll up her skirt and walk into a river. *Oh my gosh,*

he says. *She didn't have to do that.* Cars zoom across from me,
motorbikes too. Kicked-up dust coats my food,

my face. The family next door having dinner at their shop,
they wonder at me sitting so fancy on a restaurant patio

alone and if I'll be okay, am I enjoying my foreign food
across from the bar where locals play pool. Actually,

they want to know if I'm Khmer or not.
My table covered in white, fine dining in Siem Reap.

Look at me get up when the waiter comes out with water,
I'm heading for the bathroom past the chef—*Are you okay?*

—vomiting on my shoes before I reach the toilet.
The steak is rare. *Was it the pollution? Will you write a good review?*

It was the foie gras, Pierre! Shut up!
I'd rather help an orphan girl carrying her sister,

at least she'd lie to me on Pub Street, *I don't want money,*
I don't want money. I want powdered milk.

The Death of Pol Pot

I

My mother shoos us away
but I listen by the door.

There are rumors of a black snake
in the basement. It is 1998.

The adults watch the news upstairs.
On the screen, an old man is dying in his bed.

The adults are talking
loudly, two feet away from each other.

From their voices, I can tell their hatred
for that old man, a thin blanket to his chin.

II

I crawl out of a giant steaming pot
snickering to my brother.

He always plays the victim.
I love to do the evil laugh.

My brother stumbles into a tent
made from plastic chairs and a faux-fur blanket.

Nobody knows I am the villain
because when I snap my fingers

I turn into a teacup
or a wooden chair painted red.

The Radio Brings News

When I told lies, he says, the grass grew
so fast, it hid the whole field. The river
drowned the men with guns
and flowers wilted over their bodies
in apology. But nothing happened
if the lie wasn't good enough, like
when I said I love my country, I love
my people, I want to be a communist too.
And I'd raise my axe and hack the dirt
for my spoon of rice, for my cup of soup.
The river was clear, the river was fresh.
If only I was a log, if only I was a bird.
I would have freed myself.
Once a soldier asked me why I worked
so hard. His uniform nice, I lied to him
and pounded my fist to my chest and then
he left me alone. At night the radio
crackled, and someone dimmed the volume
so fast you might have thought
the sound of static was grass growing.
In the dark, I listened closely. I thought
I heard escape. I thought I heard Thailand.
I thought I heard the soldier asking me
if I wanted to run away with him
and five others tonight. If I wanted to eat.

Windfall

The fishermen, desperate, poisoned them with a cloudy gasoline
so they dropped like apples to the ground underneath a tree.

Except these were birds out of water, the conservationist said.
Sarus cranes, their long legs still wet, were sold for $200 each

at the border market, where Thais bought them and turned around.
After the war, that was how the local villagers made money.

The cranes, near extinction, migrated to waters near a Khmer Rouge holding,
where no one dared go, not that a mandate said keep out, no sign written

in blood. They rationed their food, knowing the pendulum of war
could swing anytime, and they'd need something to eat before evacuating.

They were sure it wasn't over. Invisible the egrets and ibises, invisible
the forests of the eastern border to the one they shared with Laos.

This is why the wind blows a drought hard across the land, tonnage of life
destroyed in the invisible, invisible land.

Song of an Orphaned Soldier Clearing Land Mines

When I saw my father walking I kicked the road,
convinced metal brains at his feet
the humming they heard was a knife cutting,
not a living man's voice.
They believed me. Like snakes in grass
they clicked their tongues. The gods I met
promised me they could make a life happen
after what had happened
if I knew who my father was.
I clapped my hands to signal a stream
and my father followed my sound.
He drank and bathed as I cleared the land mines
and I hoped it was him. He slept
in the jungle, dreamed jaguars circling
though it was nothing but fire burning.

Close to the Bassac, I climbed mango trees
to feed him. Along the way,
I waved my arms *no*. To himself my father said, *Yes*.
No, I did not bury the bodies
nobody had prayed for. There are things in this world
we must make one another see. My father
took me gently, each one of us
gently, he took us to the flames humming *my children,*
my children. Three provinces, I traveled with him
like this, only to take him back to Prek Eng
where he found his sisters.

If my father were to tell this, he would tell you
he carried me over his shoulders to a nearby village,
that no danger touched him
and that the gods were watching,
they wanted to see me live.

II

Tuol Sleng

Street houses and shops,
dirt roads gathered with rocks,
and above, gray palm trees.
Vendors with machetes on blocks of ice,
a wagon of green coconuts,
hand-cranking machines for sugarcane.

In this same place,
did they kill Yuos Samon?
We know they dented metal bed frames,
chained prisoners in schoolrooms.
Before the slow act of torture
each prisoner's photo was taken
with a film camera. Flash.
And now the screeching wagon wheels
hauling green coconuts,
stalks of sugarcane nearby.

*

I come here with my six-year-old nephew, Ratanak, and two neighborhood girls. My nephew sprints down the halls, ducks his head into every classroom, then off again as though he hears a school bell ring. "You see that boy running in the halls?" a tourist says to another tourist. "Does he have any respect for history?"

*

Alone inside a classroom,
instead of desks, a bed frame,
its metal slats rusted, a hammer and some chains
at the corner. The floor flecked with blood
and the walls the color.

I walk to the chalkboard,
a small piece of chalk still there,
a scribble of Khmer on the dusty board.
And numbers. I can't understand anything
but the numbers.

Meanwhile, in the courtyard,
a boy plays
as if on a playground. Rope
hangs from a high wooden frame.
Below he fills an urn with water,
takes someone prisoner,
and bobs his head with rope.
He plunges the head
and the legs struggle upside down.
He is just a boy.

*

In Lancaster by the cornfields
one afternoon,
to the clopping of a horse's hooves across the way,
I thought of Tuol Sleng.
In family portraits, I'd blink at the flash of a camera
and not be able to see after
inside a lighted room
without red invading my eyes.
That same flash
capturing the smiles of my surviving relatives.
Before Samon was murdered,
my aunt says, he had been studying at West Point
with other lieutenant generals of Lon Nol.
But maybe it was Fort Worth,
not West Point, or like many foreign troops
trained on US soil, Fort Benning.

No way of knowing,
except for this photograph:
each man smiling around the table,
a white man at the head,
a blond, curly-haired girl sitting in his lap.

This picture of my uncle hangs
in my grandmother's house, he turns to look at us.

*

A boy runs through the halls of Tuol Sleng,
his narrow footsteps turn it back into a school.
He checks every classroom for the other kids.
He sits on a chair and waits. When I walk in,
he whispers, *ghost*. The bell rings and off he goes.

*

Still my nephew speeds down the halls,
peeking his head into every room.

Ratanak, I call out, *stop running. Stop.* I say,
Don't make me count. He knows

but he doesn't know—*One*—this was once
a torture prison, now a museum—

Two—though to him, it's just an old school,
which is why he's running, which is why

inside a sepia-toned cell—*Three*—
he's lost and waits for me.

*

Visitors to Cambodia, who wander around
with crushed limes in their sugarcane drinks,
can say people of this country
suffered so much but are so happy.

Years later, alone in Phnom Penh,
I think of my uncle, whom I did not know,
and imagine him returning from the US,
taken at the airport.

And I think of how my mother,
washing dishes bordered with gray flowers,
sobbed over the sink and spoke.

I don't know what happened to my brother.
His wife and sons pleaded with him to come home.

So heartbroken your grandmother
when she learned the news about my brother,

hoping, all this time, he'd been waiting for us in another
country, only to find out that he died alone.

Of all the photographs at Tuol Sleng, not one of my brother.
That day we couldn't find his face, we went home.

*

I explain to Ratanak:

The tourists are here to stroke black-and-white photographs
of tortured prisoners.
They press closer to look at a picture:
a handcuffed boy
leaning toward them. Walking slow
around the prison,
they crouch in cramped stalls and shut themselves in
to imagine what horrors.

They walk around the metal bed frame,
cover their mouths at rusted chains,
the hammer and toolbox in the corner,
the floor stained
and the walls the color.
They cry. They write on the walls NEVER FORGET
signing their names.
Now they have been here.
They buy books from the souvenir shops
and silk scarves and krama
and handmade purses.

But we come here to look for someone.

*

The boy is still inside a classroom.
He raises his hand to answer the teacher's question.
The teacher offers him a turn at the board
and gives him a piece of chalk.
His back is turned to the other students.
Now the teacher is a soldier.
Now the boy has chains on his wrists.
Now he's smacked in the face.
Now his glasses break on his nose bridge.
Now he pretends he cannot spell
or count how many teeth knocked out.

*

Already the tourists have forgotten while sucking sugar from cane
as they head to the Royal Palace
for the rest of their tour.

But I still stand by the prison entrance
with the apparition of a boy who cannot point to me
where my uncle died.

Look at them shaking their heads at Ratanak.
I turn around to find my nephew.

He is running again. The girls follow him,
and now I chase after them into the schoolyard.

III

In a Room of One Thousand Buddhas

The water in my heart was falling. To my right
a row of Buddhas in meditation
sheltered by the Naga snake but this snake was real,
unlike the American and the heads in his cabinet.
The Naga protected the Buddha from rain,
spread its seven hoods to keep him dry.
And did I tell you it was raining all day?
I bought a poncho to ride around Siem Reap.
Rain during the dry season. Buddha calling on the earth
for witness. Something water protectors
at Standing Rock are doing right now. Protecting water
because water is life. But a night of rubber bullets
and tear gas and water hoses, that is not life.
Today, too, while I ate breakfast noodles in my hotel
neo-Nazis saluted back home in Harrisburg.
They were not calling on the earth, their palms up
but facing down. Looking at the Buddhas,
I thought, *They look like me.*
Some with broader shoulders, some from pre-Angkorian
and Angkorian times, some from this century,
four sitting back to back in a circle,
each in different mudras. Sandstone. Wood. Stone.
Depending on what was available
or how kings chose to perpetuate who they worshipped.
Sitting on the coils of the Naga. Eyes closed.
Or looking down. Some look scared. Calm.
Some with hands missing or cracked down the side.
Some look starved. Their clothes shattered.
One, wooden, was defaced standing.
Except for a small curve of lip and one shut left eye.
There are others, smaller, small as people.

Cruel Radiance

I take the R from 86th St to teach poetry
in Manhattan. My hands sweat
on *Cruel Radiance*. The front cover: photograph of a girl

the Khmer Rouge executed, one of many
children presumed *counterrevolutionary enemies,*
as the soiled descendants of such. My chest heaves. To everyone

on the train I do not say, All the sobbing inside of me,
all of it you know now! But you don't know
what I am called! Aneakajun—traitor of my roots.

Instead, I catch the N across the platform, continue
reading about S-21. *We were not inside*
those prisons: they were. Our hells

almost certainly are not theirs. A white girl
with a streak of blue hair falls flat
on her back. Her head a bowling ball

close to my foot. Her head a bowling ball that rolls
on the floor. I look up
from reading *cozy existential atmosphere* (Adorno's

words) and there, a white girl on the ground—
breathing, breathing. Breathing.
Someone call 911! Someone press the emergency button!

Someone pull the girl up! Now
she is sitting, telling someone she's on her way
to 23rd St as the train screeches to my stop on 8th.

Doors open. I see how *the distinction between*
victim and executioner becomes blurred.
I want to cancel class. Because why? So I can sob

about the killing fields and how aneakajun feels?
I'd rather do that today. My head could be a bowling ball too.
I could fall over from this too.

ABC for Refugees

Cherub-bee-dee how does a man
who doesn't read English well know that cherub-bee-dum
those aren't really words-bee-dee.
But birds.

Cherub-bee-dum, he stumbles, reading to me
by the sliding glass door cherub-bee-dee, through which I watch
my brother play in the dum-dum-yard.

Cherub-bee-dee, cherub-bee-dum, like how my father says
Fine then! Leave! My mother shouts, *Stupid! Dumb!*
We live in a small bee-dee-nest too, one hallway to bee-dum-slam doors

Birds? What are birds?
Thanks to my father, reading with me, I have more feathers.

T-H-E. First word he ever taught me to pluck. . .
It is a word used all the time. Cherub-cherub-bee-dum!

The mail. *The* mailbox. *The* school bus. *The the.*

He asks me to read the mail. Not birds, *mail.*
If you don't read this, you will turn into birds.
And I read it to him the best I can.
The end. A feather. Two feathers. The. The end.

Mother, mother. Repeat after me.
Cherub-bee-dee, cherub-bee-dum!
We read together before bedtime.

Ode to the Loom

Dear loom, dear box skeleton,
special ordered and
handcrafted from wood,
you rest on the floor
and wait for her
to sit down with you
and together weave
fabrics for weddings
between lovers and warriors,
the survivors, surviving.
Your sturdy frame
animates her as living
portrait, simple as the chain
on her glasses, the calm focus:
steady hands on the shuttle,
the weft and the warp,
feet on the treadle.
You obey the soft sheen
of turquoise, cherry, and gold
wrapped at the body's waist,
your gift to the body,
hundreds of bodies for the new year,
for the blessings of ancestors.
Sweet loom, old friend of an old woman,
you are an ancestor she prays to,
so that when her hair falls
not as rain does
but as nails the evening hangs on,
and her hands slip no longer
from silk but on walls in the dark
hall to her room,

her daughters will sadly dismantle you,
remnant of a lost home, sacred language
coded inside her native language.
When she passes,
you will be stowed away
in the basement.
You will remind us of her,
you, loom, who have kept her company,
nonjudgmental witness to her secrets.
You will remember best
the way she works, the spots on her legs,
her bare toes peeking
from the edge of her sarong,
the slow motion of her hand
slapping flies in summertime
or the sound of gorges rushed
from her face in the quiet hours of the cloth
when she was depressed, she was depressed—
she pressed against you daily and wept.

I Am Rachana

My husband is the last historian. The others were found out by Angkar early on, taken beyond fields, to black holes, dark corners of temples, some say, to Ratanakiri, then thrown into Laos, some say. Nobody can know they were our friends, not now, not in Year Zero. Now alone, he can't help his research. I hear him in secret: a pointed stick lightly scratching peeled bark, swirling ashes from under the cooking pot. What he writes, he memorizes, erases, recites the next day. His song of labyrinths stops when a spy passes our hut. How is it? They have the many eyes of a pineapple. And my husband suddenly blows smoke into a pile of leaves into wood, he burns a dangerous light. Still watching, the comrade passes. He waits to begin again. If Angkar caught him writing, you know what would happen to both of us. I hold on to a memory: I used to make samlar machu, used to cut the skin of a pineapple and toss it in soup.

Cambodia

In these fields, nothing talks. Nothing. Nothing.
Nothing laughs.

Mosquitoes live longer, as long as trees. The jaws
of mosquitoes will sting children who belong to their parents, and the girl
who runs to the hut where her family eats
will be greeted by vultures,
worshipped in the temple
where children don't sleep.

Nothing eats in these fields. Nothing. Nothing.
Nothing drinks.
In Tonle Sap far off: a bloated face inside
a blue plastic bag wishes to see the sky,
and so opens its eyes, and that old man
        they whip all night
can't get up; this is why
they tie his hands to a krasang tree.

This real life is a story!
Life! Life! We sleep
in bed at night
but do not story a story because life!

The Death of Henry Kissinger

Bubbles children blow toward the sky
burst bombs into jasmine.
Anything that flies on anything that moves.

You got that? Got that. Roger that.
And a mother's golden lotus bud
orbiting her daughter's neck?

Perhaps a giant kite to block B-52s?
Balloons from my birthday party
to bring on your jets? Go ahead.

I dare you to send submarines too.
To add: *Anything that swims.* Your idea
of swimming is not dreaming is not flight.

But in Takeo, at the edge of the forest,
if a spot-billed duck were to lay an egg.
Well. It would be bad for you.

Do you copy? Do you read me?
Blue, speckled egg. Rebirth as revenge.
It's an order. It's to be done. Over. And out.

Self-Portrait as War Museum Captions

A daughter of survivors stands in the grass among tattered military tanks. She is the only one in her family who wants to visit the museum. Siem Reap, Cambodia. Nov 2016.

"Loud little weed eater." A worker cuts the grass and the noise activates the scene of a battlefield.

An Australian girl screams, Mum I want a bazooka! as a Japanese tourist picks up an AK-47 on display. In broken Khmer, the woman asks a museum guide/former Khmer Rouge soldier, "Why do you allow tourists to play with guns?" He smiles.

"Triggered." The young woman hurries away from photos of the evacuation, bumps into a row of USSR armored cars.

The woman swiftly turns, jumps at a muzzle that greets her at eye level. Howitzer 105mm. M2A2. Artillery made in USA in 1953.

Closer, a lawn mower eats around the land mine exhibit.

The young woman rests next to a DK 75mm made in China, found in Anlong Veng.

The Woman Who Was Small, Not Because the World Expanded

The elephants came
out from the fields
and carried me toward Chambak,
toward a village doused in fires,
so that in the pond
fish had fried,
and looking at that dead water
was a woman
I had seen running home
each evening with a bucket
in her hand.
Always her speed was the hair
that flew in my face.
Always her feet sounding of tanks
which made dogs bark and flee,
footprints deep as trenches
in the grass.
This is the woman
who had shrunk
so small
when the planes came,
nobody could ever find her.
And since more planes,
she stayed as small
as a spoon,
and the world seemed to enlarge
though nothing had changed,
and when she saw me
she hid, threw pebbles at my ankles
until I bowed down
and easily picked her up
folding her inside a banana leaf.

She slept. She slept well—
she who is my mother
sleeping off the world again,
whose person
I hold in my hand
when she wants to be held.

Here Is Your Name

Here's where you first wrote your name
next to your brother writing his name
next to your mother and your father
who both have their own names.
Here's your family watching you
trying to write your name, you erasing,
the new eraser whittled down.
Here's the composition paper shifting
underneath your left hand, your right hand
striking out and your brother yawning.
Here are your hands awake
in the middle of the night, your fingers
turn on the lamp, your whole hand
wrapped around a pencil,
nobody hovering over you,
the pencil crossing out the page, the zigzag
of an M upright, not sideways for Mama,
Mak, Srei Mol, Ming Dute, Bong Molyden,
Mokkie, and Mikey, M like how your mother
says, *Don't call me Mak, call me Mai,*
like how your brother and you play
　　　　Mother May I—

Here's the side of the white leather sofa
where you wrote your name in pen
when guests were in the living room.
Here's you writing your brother's name
next to yours, as he played outside with friends,
here are the guests telling your father on you,
your father at the dinner table, saying,
Repeat after me: slabaprea, sam, kabet.

Here's the spoon, fork, and knife
to eat your mother's samlar kakou.
Here's you saying *spoon, fork,* and *knife*
instead of what your father said.
Here are your brother's insides shaking
and you cracking up with him.
Here's your father clearing his plate
and leaving the room. Here's you
at the table, after listening to the radio,
singing, *Bad bad bad bad*
boy! You make me feel so good—
your father asking, *Ha? Ta mek?* You saying,
It's a song, Dad. Here are his lips
tightening and the *Go to your room*
and you going or else the orange flyswatter.

Here's your brother whining, *Mom, I'm thirsty.*
Your mother sitting in the driver's seat in July,
you and your brother in the backseat.
Here's your mother without any water
in the stranded car. Here's your mouth
half full of saliva and the tap-tap
on your brother's shoulder to help.
Here's your brother saying, *That's not water.*
That's spit. Here's your brother climbing
the backyard maple, on the highest branch,
reaching for the highest twig
because the neighborhood kids dared him
and here's you on the patio,
telling him, *Come down, come down now.*
Here's your brother backing down
branch by branch. Here you are,
afraid you will fall, your brother pushing himself

up the temple, you are following your brother
up the temple, until both of you sit at the top,
out of breath, above the land, the window
breezing through you everything dirt and green.
Here's your brother pointing at the salamander
that scurried across the ceiling,
your brother sweating on the trail
to the zoo, where the monkeys chased him
for his bag of peanuts, the photo of you
and your brother resting on the steps of
Angkor Wat, both of you looking down
at your mother's sun hat, your father's shades.
Here your brother asks to drink your water
and though you said yes, you
slap the bottle out of his hand.

Your brother will not go back
and here you are back again.
Your relatives ask, *Where is your brother?*
You say, *He's coming next time.*
But he's still up there in that tree
and here you are still writing your name
and your brother's name, now your mother's
and father's names, as though writing them
might make your names true.

Notes

The cover photograph is of traditional Cambodian silk woven by my grandmother, Bun Em, a master weaver who was recognized with a National Heritage Fellowship from the National Endowment for the Arts in 1990.

"Americans Dancing in the Heart of Darkness" describes the tragic human stampede that happened in Phnom Penh during Bon Om Touk on November 22, 2010.

In "The Radio Host Goes into Hiding," the lines "like water to survive / I must hold on to / an individual idea / to keep strong because to be reeducated is to be destroyed" are from the documentary *The Missing Picture* by Rithy Panh. The poem also refers to the singer Yol Aularong and is influenced by the documentary *Don't Think I've Forgotten: Cambodia's Lost Rock and Roll* by John Pirozzi.

"Sestina" is dedicated to my mother, Thoch Yuos, and her sisters, Pech, Pam, and Lynn Yuos.

"The Radio Brings News" is a persona poem dedicated to my father, Sarith Sok.

"Tuol Sleng" is set in the Tuol Sleng Genocide Museum, the site of former Chao Ponhea Yat High School, which the Khmer Rouge used as the notorious S-21 execution center from 1975 to 1979.

"In a Room of One Thousand Buddhas" takes place in Angkor National Museum in Siem Reap.

In "Cruel Radiance," the italicized sentences are from *The Cruel Radiance: Photography and Political Violence* by Susie Linfield.

In "Cambodia," the repetition is inspired by Federico García Lorca's "City That Does Not Sleep."

In "The Death of Henry Kissinger," the italicized sentences are from a conversation between Henry Kissinger and Alexander Haig. The full quotation refers to Richard Nixon: "He wants a massive bombing campaign in Cambodia. He doesn't want to hear anything. It's an order, it's to be done. Anything that flies, on anything that moves. You got that?" (National Security Archive Electronic Briefing Book No. 123)

"Self-Portrait as War Museum Captions" takes place at the War Museum Cambodia in Siem Reap.

"Here Is Your Name" is dedicated to my brother, Ramo, and my cousins, Youthana, Bunnawatt, Kamarin, Jessica, Samantha, Toby, and Cody.

Acknowledgments

Thank you to the editors of the following journals and magazines
in which these poems, sometimes in earlier versions, first appeared:
*The Adroit Journal, Boston Review, Consequence Magazine, FIELD,
The Georgia Review, Hyperallergic, Kenyon Review, Narrative,
The New Republic, Ninth Letter, The Offing, Poetry, Poetry
International, The Rumpus,* and *TriQuarterly.* Thanks to the
following anthologies for including my poetry: *Resistance, Rebellion,
Life: 50 Poems Now,* and *The World I Leave You: Asian American
Poets on Faith and Spirit.* Many poems also appeared in the
chapbook *Year Zero,* winner of a Poetry Society of America
Chapbook Fellowship 30 and Under, selected by Marilyn Chin.

I am grateful for the journey and the support of the NYU Creative
Writing Program, Kundiman, the Community of Writers at Squaw
Valley, the Napa Valley Writers' Conference, the Bread Loaf
Writers' Conference, Barbara Deming Memorial Fund, the Elizabeth
George Foundation, the Jerome Foundation, the MacDowell Colony,
Hedgebrook, Saltonstall Foundation for the Arts, the National
Endowment for the Arts, the Fine Arts Work Center Summer
Workshops, The Conversation Literary Festival, the Kundiman
residence at Sierra Nevada College, Montalvo Arts Center, 92nd
Street Y Unterberg Poetry Center, The Ruby in San Francisco, and
the Wallace Stegner Program at Stanford University. Thanks to all
the wonderful people I met along the way.

I have so much reverence for my teachers and those who have
offered me insight: Kimiko Hahn, Sharon Olds, Brenda Shaughnessy,
Deborah Landau, Eavan Boland, David Keplinger, Ilya Kaminsky,
Carl Phillips, and Bruce Weigl. Special thanks to Yusef Komunyakaa
who salvaged the line that became the title of this book.

Thanks to those who dreamed with me in my time of need. Thanks
for seeing me through all the changes: Marwa Helal, Charleen

McClure, Ashley Jones, Chen Chen, Danny Thanh Nguyen, Angela So, Kimarlee Nguyen, Mai-Linh Hong, Chinelo Okparanta, Peter Pa, Charif Shanahan, Paul Tran, Hieu Minh Nguyen, Javier Zamora, Emily Jungmin Yoon, sam sax, Khaty Xiong, Nabila Lovelace, Jeremiah Headen, Laura Jew, and Youthana Yuos.

Thanks to my community in Oakland for holding me with such tenderness, especially Banteay Srei and the Center for Empowering Refugees and Immigrants.

This book would not be possible without sisterhood and the generational wisdom of the women of color who affirmed me throughout my experiences. To all of you who told me, *You're enough:* Thank you, I know. You are enough.

My gratitude stretches to infinity for my ancestors who are always in the room—especially my grandmother Bun Em, whose own hands helped me weave this book; for my aunts, uncles, and cousins in Prek Eng, Phnom Penh, Kandal, Takeo, Philly, and Harrisburg— you make me want to thrive wherever I am; and finally, for my origin story—Mom, Dad, and Ramo, with whom I began to form language, and from language, love.

About the Author

Monica Sok is a Cambodian American poet and the daughter of former refugees. Her work has been recognized with a Discovery Prize from the 92nd Street Y Unterberg Poetry Center. She is the recipient of fellowships from Hedgebrook, the Elizabeth George Foundation, the National Endowment for the Arts, Kundiman, the Jerome Foundation, the MacDowell Colony, Saltonstall Foundation for the Arts, and others. Currently, Sok is a 2018–20 Wallace Stegner Fellow at Stanford University and also teaches poetry at the Center for Empowering Refugees and Immigrants and Banteay Srei in Oakland, California. She is originally from Lancaster, Pennsylvania.

Poetry is vital to language and living. Since 1972, Copper Canyon Press has published extraordinary poetry from around the world to engage the imaginations and intellects of readers, writers, booksellers, librarians, teachers, students, and donors.

WE ARE GRATEFUL FOR THE MAJOR SUPPORT PROVIDED BY:

THE PAUL G. ALLEN
FAMILY FOUNDATION

CULTURE

the point
envision·enact·evolve

Anonymous

Jill Baker and Jeffrey Bishop

Anne and Geoffrey Barker

Donna and Matt Bellew

Diana Broze

John R. Cahill

The Beatrice R. and Joseph A. Coleman Foundation Inc.

The Currie Family Fund

Laurie and Oskar Eustis

Saramel and Austin Evans

Mimi Gardner Gates

Gull Industries Inc. on behalf of William True

The Trust of Warren A. Gummow

Carolyn and Robert Hedin

Bruce Kahn

Phil Kovacevich and Eric Wechsler

Lakeside Industries Inc.

on behalf of Jeanne Marie Lee

Maureen Lee and Mark Busto

TO LEARN MORE ABOUT UNDERWRITING
COPPER CANYON PRESS TITLES,
PLEASE CALL 360-385-4925 EXT. 103

WE ARE GRATEFUL FOR THE MAJOR SUPPORT PROVIDED BY:

Peter Lewis

Ellie Mathews and Carl Youngmann as The North Press

Larry Mawby

Hank Meijer

Jack Nicholson

Petunia Charitable Fund and adviser Elizabeth Hebert

Gay Phinny

Suzie Rapp and Mark Hamilton

Emily and Dan Raymond

Jill and Bill Ruckelshaus

Cynthia Sears

Kim and Jeff Seely

Dan Waggoner

Randy and Joanie Woods

Barbara and Charles Wright

Caleb Young as C. Young Creative

The dedicated interns and faithful volunteers
of Copper Canyon Press

The Chinese character for poetry is made up of two parts:
"word" and "temple."
It also serves as pressmark for Copper Canyon Press.

This book is set in CMU Serif and Franklin Gothic.
Design by Katy Homans.
Printed on archival-quality paper.